BETWEEN NIGHT AND

BETWEEN NIGHT AND DANCING LIGHT

A Duet of Complementing Verse

Keith and Elizabeth Stanley-Mallett

ARTHUR H. STOCKWELL LTD
Torrs Park   Ilfracombe   Devon
Established 1898
www.ahstockwell.co.uk

British Library Cataloguing-in-Publication Data.
A catalogue record for this book is available
from the British Library.

Previously published poems by the same author:
Little Traveller – Pumpkin Publications
Conspiracy of Faculties – Poetry Now, Forward Press, 1994
Yielding Forms – Poetry Now, 1994
One, That are We – Poetry Now, 1994
Two Minutes of Silence – Anchor Books, 1994
A Norfolk Winter Sunset – Poets England Series, Brentham Press, 1994
Come Silently to Me – Poetry Now, 1995
To the Eye – Poetry Now, 1995
World Wide Conceded Nationally – Poetry Now, 1996
Three Times Twenty – Poetry Now, 1996
I Believe in Betjeman – Poetry Now, 1996
Emotive Machine – Poetry Now, 1996
Essence of Time – Poetry Now, 1996
Poetic Visions – Poetry Now, 1996
Once Upon a Time – Poetry Now, 1996
The Red Fox – Anchor Books, 1997
Soul Winds – Poetry Now, 1997
Across a Timeless Threshold – Anchor Books, 1999
Mrs Batholomew's Door – Anchor Books, 1999
Electronic Life – United Press, 1999
Under An Indigo Moon – Arthur H. Stockwell Ltd, 2009
Beneath Rose-Lemon Skies – Arthur H. Stockwell Ltd, 2009
Before the Rainbow Fades – Arthur H. Stockwell Ltd, 2010

ISBN 978-0-7223-4030-1 Paperback edition.
ISBN 978-0-7223-4031-8 Cloth-bound edition.
Printed in Great Britain by
Arthur H. Stockwell Ltd
Torrs Park   Ilfracombe
Devon

FOREWORD

BOOK IV

This book, the fourth to be published by Keith and Elizabeth Stanley-Mallett, continues their style of work.

The colour and simplicity in their poetry is to encourage those who do not generally do so to read poetry or light verse.

Between Night and Dancing Light, although not part of the previous trio published earlier, nevertheless can be included to make a quartet. Obviously each volume stands on its own individuality.

Their work, being complementary in style to a degree, creates an interesting view of life – again the book is in two parts. Part I is of verse written by Keith; Part II, poems by Elizabeth.

All poems are original and previously unpublished.

PART I

A DUET OF
COMPLEMENTING VERSE

By

Keith Stanley-Mallett

CONTENTS

Below or Above

Away up to the clouds
Through a break in the grey,
Up to the brightness
 And there who can say –

What marvels are found
High above the earth,
What sights can you see?
 From Bath to the Firth –

Is it true that the world
Looks patched like a quilt,
The seas are like puddles
 And all on a tilt –

The earth turns below
While the stars shine on high,
Just one of a kind
 With those in the sky.

Whether below, or
Above the high clouds,
Questions and answers
 Are still as profound.

Comprehension

What was it I said to you
The other day, that made you cringe
And slink away?

I did not want to hurt you,
Did not realise I had offended,
You did not say.

Will you forgive what I said
Even though I do not know?
Please can we talk.

I will make amends to you
If you review the spoken wound,
Was it my fault?

No barb was meant or meaning
And I await your dearest wishes
Alone, confused.

Yet, now I see a chink of light,
I did not offend, this was goodbye,
Just an excuse.

An Inn, in Time

The old inn stood alone
At the side of a dusty lane.
    A meeting place for local gentry
    Farmers and travellers who came –

To this sanctuary for rest,
A bottle of wine and a tale,
    Fresh bread, cheese and beef
    Or a smoke and a jug of ale.

One man leant on the stone surround
Of the large ornate fireplace,
    And others on benches sprawled
    Discussing the day and latest taste.

The smoke curled up from the long,
Stemmed pipes as they chatted on,
    Ignoring the night and the wind
    That blew, creating an eerie song.

The old inn sign, swayed in the wind,
The 'Poacher and Dog' swung creaking
    From the rusty rings of iron,
    And lamps flickered by the winds seeking.

And through the dark scudding clouds
A glimpse of a sickle moon.
    That briefly lit the darkened scene
    Of shadows, trees and witch's broom –

Caught in the light, then suddenly gone,
Leaving only the wind and rustling trees,
    Flickering lanterns and a moment
    In time, shared by those whose spirit sees.

Endeavour

Across illustrious history
Rides the glorious moments
Of revelation, change and truth
From which understanding ensues.

Those sudden brief sparks of light
Or years of belief in a theory,
The ability of men to construct
Learn, devise and instruct –

Others, the work to progress
On to a final far honing,
Developing mind and condition
To a successful fruition.

Each theory and principal
Hard learnt, forms histories
Foundation for each rung on the ladder,
And humanity's continued endeavour.

The Fabric of Reality

If, when an ill stage is set
And all comes strangely together,
At a time and spot
Chosen by chance or eldritch weather,
Should you find yourself alone,
Bemused, in a darkened place,
Where light is most dim
Weird of hue with everything waste,
Then you have reached that plain
That land, the nether space,
Whose surreal unliving sight
Features a nothing face.
Beware of shapes and murmuring voice
And unseen hands that pull,
Colours that slowly merge
Bewitching, a trap to fool.
Is this perchance a dream you're in,
A nightmare, or a shift
In time or dimension,
It is I believe a rift
In the fabric of reality
You must take the utmost care,
For all I can offer you now
Is a prayer, you do not linger there.

'Til Crowing

I sit here in the heat
　　　　A-glowing,
Electric fan switched on
　　　　Full-blowing,
Hair in the draught
　　　　A-flowing,
Waiting for the hot sun
　　　　A-going.
For with the cooling air
　　　　A-showing,
Temperatures of the day
　　　　Lowering,
I then will lift my glass
　　　　Full knowing,
I may cool my brow
　　　　'Til crowing,
Of a new hot dawn
　　　　A-glowing.

Defiant

*L*ife looks down upon the verdant
Isle of Britain,
In this year two thousand and nine
Upon a diminishing green,
A land of shame.
Little enough of green is left
And of forest,
Likewise little of the proud name
Once held in the greatest respect,
Now the sorriest.
Of all the great noble nations
Great Britain now,
Has lost her once historic way
Made worse by ill-meaning leaders
And traitors foul.
Much is made of modern progress
Concrete and roads,
That will never renew the splendour,
It takes the right people to govern,
Those who once showed
A tenacity for freedom,
Self-reliant,
The British want Great Britain
In the hands of those who will make
A land, defiant!

Depths of Night

Moonlight and shadows
    The night enfolds,
Rustling and whispering
    A strangeness holds.

What denizens of night
    Are out and about,
From gloom of the woods
    And old grassy mounts.

A-creeping along
    The hedgerows stark,
Or slinking in slimy
    Cold waters dark.

What strange creatures
    Skulk without lanterns?
Witches and goblins
    And ghostly phantoms.

Is it all in the mind?
    One never knows,
When, in the depths of night
    The fear starts to grow.

Cap-a-Pie

Armed cap-a-pie
    In steel and leather,
The soldiers of old
    Went together –

To fight their day-long
    Battles, for a lord,
With armoured horse
    Shield and sword.

They cut and thrust with
    Axe, spear and bow
A great melee they formed
    And the blood did flow.

They did not die for God
    They did not die for good,
But they died in thousands
    As good soldiers should –

For a reputation,
    A castle or land,
What good in the end
    Just bloodlust in man.

A Garden Memory

There's a little half-hidden
                    Garden,
At the end of a small lane
                    Charming,
Once, before they took away
                    The line,
Where the old railway did run
                    Were fine
Old cottages and smithy,
                    Now gone,
Leaving just this remnant
                    Upon
The memory, the garden
                    Itself,
A haven of rich fruit trees,
                    A wealth
Of scented shrub, and flower,
                    Fallen
Now, a patch of neglected
                    Forgotten
Life, tangled undergrowth with
                    Bramble
Overgrown rose, plum, sloe, and
                    Ambles
There, only squirrel and crow.

Timeless Spirit

Where does the spirit go to play
    When it leaves this earth of clay.

Into darkened worlds unknown
    A land of shadows shown,

Or down beneath all below
    To the caverns all aglow.

Perhaps to float, drifting free
    With each caressing breeze –

Like unto faerie realms
    Of elemental elves,

Surely not as ghostly shades
    Invisible or frightening made?

Could it be we play afar
    Amongst the distant stars,

A timeless spirit's voyage
    To everlasting knowledge.

September Night

When September beckons autumn
And days begin to shorten,
Slowly, the night broadens
Tightening the darkening cordon.

Aware of change, birds drift away
Earlier in the evening,
To tree, perch, or nest to rest
Unseen and unseeing –

Hidden, silent, for lengthening hours
While rabbits play hide and seek
On meadows by running hedges,
And bats flit without sound or beat.

Bewitching moonlight floods
Through broken cloud to reveal,
Black and even blacker shadows
Amidst the pale-white shade surreal.

Yet, this September night will pass
Dew will soak the fields of grass,
And bright, the morning star fast
Heralds the coming dawn, at last.

The Very Thought

Will the amplified vox humana
    Ever quieten or still,
This modern wail and moan of voice
    Of unheard words that fill –

The very air, in radio waves
    A constant media background,
To all and everything presented
    Each concert that pounds.

What is so attractive about noise
    Without harmony or melody,
Played so loudly, it contorts
    The very notes, the very keys –

To a cacophony of sound
    That attacks the senses' feelings,
And betrays the very thought
    Of music, as understood the meaning.

Currents of Air

Currents of air
Currents of air
Created by
  Temperatures –

Where, cold meets
Hot, starting
The wind that drives,
  Hot flows up –

Cold forced down
Becoming strong
Whirling round,
  Soon to widen –

Expanding far
Over oceans
Land and mountain
  Gathering speed –

Travelling fast
Becomes a gale
Strong to feed,
  Thus to a storm –

Or tempest grows.
Who would expect
What air could form
  When currents are born?

The Sanity?

Where in the human heart
　　Is found mercy?
Where in the human mind
　　The sanity?
Where in the human brain
　　Understanding?
Where in human senses
　　Is the damning?

Therein we have flawed
　　Intelligence,
Therein we are unstable
　　Yet still content,
Therein we go to war,
　　And not debate,
Therefore we must learn
　　Before it's too late.

A Summer's Sigh

The sun rides high
Above wind-blown clouds,
    Reflecting light across the sky
    From bright-lit shrouds.

As they in turn
Slowly change in form,
    Morphing into ships and dragons
    Riding out the storm –

To drift away
On wind-torn silence,
    Seeking the shadowed horizons
    Beckoning distance.

Slowly the cloak
Leaves a clearing sky,
    From which, flows a flood of gold
    Like a summer's sigh.

Just a Big Head

Old Mr Dumpty
Was a big head,
But did he know
He was only an egg?

Most of the time
He just sat on a wall
I wonder, did
He not think he could fall?

Believe you me
If old Humpty did fall,
King's men, soldiers,
All the short and the tall –

Butchers, bakers
And barbers as doctors,
None could repair
An egg, which had dropped or –

Fallen off walls,
This old character's
Still alive in rhymes
The nurseries captured.

By Flash and Flare

It is, its very own nature
  That flashes and flares
Across the dark unknowing,
  Sparking bright thoughts, rare.

The unseeing, unknowing
  Like a void, silent,
The mental spirit gathers
  Nothing, projects faint –

Theoretical thoughts to the air
  Yet if the mind fails,
To brightly thrust and penetrate
  The unreasoned veil –

That hangs before enlightenment
  Nothing can be shared,
Until the mind is ignited
  By that flash and flare –

Of coalescing truth that now
  Shows the path the quest,
Opening the eyes to free
  Knowledge from darkness.

Autumn Smoke

The bonfire smoke curls up
Into an early autumn sky,
    Drifting over the hedgerow
    And the willow trees nearby.

An evening breeze fans the smoke
Away across the gardens,
    Leaving that sweet pungent smell
    That accompanies autumn.

The hot bright days of summer
Replaced now, by a softer
    Mellow light, falls quieter,
    Caressing the late blossom.

Wine

To rest is to taste the wine of ease
To sleep is to taste refreshing wine,

To dream, is to taste the wine of fantasy
To love, is to drink the wine of life.

You may drink the sparkling wines
Of the vineyards near and far,

But wine will never taste as good
As love's own wine, sweet as cinnabar.

Tea in a Field

Screw the lid on tightly, Emma,
    For the wasps are about today,
After the jam, cream and sugar
    And they're getting in the way.

It's so good to have a picnic
    In the countryside at last,
Sitting in the sun eating,
    Sandwiches on the grass.

The kettle's singing nicely
    On the old methylated stove.
The cups and cakes are ready
    Or lemonade if you chose.

Once we've had a game or two
    And chased the rabbits to the hedge,
We'll have to pack the picnic up
    And leave for home and bed.

Too Hot

It's not that I want to leave you
    But the sun's too hot for me,
Look at my Chocolate Orange
    All gooey and sticky.
It's all right for the grown-ups
    They just don't seem to care,
With refrigerated cold drinks
    Sun-glasses and deck-chairs.

It's far too hot for any games
    And I'm getting rather thirsty,
We'll go into the kitchen
    Because, we are rather dirty,
It's the kitchen tap for a splash,
    Then, with cold drinks to cool us down
We'll go and watch the tele,
    Who wants to turn pink, red or brown?

Of the Wild

Fox-red, fox-fur,
Fox-sharp, fox-sleek,
Fox-den, fox-cub,
Fox-run, fox-fleet.

The fox, his life
Is fear and stress,
To run from horse
And hounds of death.

He's not a pet
Of that we know,
He's of the wild
And all a-lone.

He should be left
His life to own,
There's far more crime
In us, we're shown.

The Night Advances

When the last bloom of sunset's
   Glowing rose-gold fire,
   Meets the deepening blue of night
   Then bats flit, from barn and byre
Beyond the dark-mouthed trees,
   Whose open arms hide shadows
   Deep, darker even than the night,
   Yet light still falls upon the meadows,
Cast by a sylvan sickle moon
   That plays hide and seek with swift
   Floating clouds, drawn like patched
   Coverlets, which, to far horizons drift,
Below a salted sky of early stars
   The darkened night advances,
   While flit of bat, hoot of owl,
   Bark of fox, spells a night enchanted.

What Is, This Time?

The wheel of time
    Spins round and round,
Never to stop
    And this confounds,
The minds of most
    Who know not what,
To think or say
    Of space-time's lot,
And is it best
    Not to worry,
Nothing stops time
    So let's hurry,
And have some fun
    Before the wheel,
Spins on around
    Our lives to steal,
Let those who can
    That have the time,
Study the wheel
    To find the sign,
That thus explains
    As old Einstein,
And tells them just
    What is, this time?

This Singular Beauty

A black silhouette
Stands in symmetrical
Perfection, against
The rose-blush evening sky,

The tree, a landmark,
Stands upon high ground
A sentinel stark,
Of such natural art –

That no brush of paint
Upon any canvas,
Could equal in merit
This singular beauty –

This living plant life,
Etched against a sky
Magnificent of hue,
Creating this picture, true.

Clear and Bright

Tell me, dear reader,
I'd like your view,
Objectively
On poetry that's clear to you,

Conversely also
When you peruse,
Subjectively
Verse that's clear, written true –

Writ not to confound
Or contort that
Subject matter,
Which is the focus in fact –

Of all written verse
That the reader,
Must interpret
Decisively by him or her –

And thus poetry
Should be clear and bright,
To the reader
For whom the writer writes.

Gateway to Winter

The corn has been cut
The hedgerow's preceding,
The trees to gold turning
The cold is now creeping.

The squirrels collecting
The rabbits are hiding,
The wind is keening
The clouds are riding.

The sun is paling
The sky is darkening,
The lamps glimmer early
The fox sounds his barking.

The autumn draws in
The season of change,
The gateway to winter,
The year slowly wanes.

Truth of Mind

Do you own your own mind?
Is it really your own?
Or has a subtle invasion taken place
    Where ideas not your own, have grown,

Can you rely on self,
That your beliefs are yours,
Formulated by reasoning that sought
    For answers to which you concur, wrought –

By defining truth
From fiction or the false,
By study of subject matter or form,
    Or philosophy to determine what course.

All such paths lead to where
Ideas are personally
Nursed to eventual fruition,
    That changes thought, views, unknowingly.

Do you really understand
The thoughts within your head,
Believe they're truly your very own
    Or are you by subtlety, being led?

A Country Picture

Sheep on the high ground
    Cows in the meadow,
Ponies by the woodland
    Keeping in the shadow.

Corn by the hayfields
    Potatoes in rows,
Cabbages full green
    Abundantly grow.

Orchards in the valley
    Apple, plum and pear,
Soft fruits in gardens
    Of the market, share.

Chickens in the yard
    Ducks and geese beyond,
Strutting in the warmth
    Dipping in the pond.

Green fields and hedgerows
    Trees that shade from light,
Meandering streams
    Running fresh and bright.

Profound, Beguiling or Banal

Is this life of ours profound?
What is this normality?
Living on this earthly ground
Beguiling or banal see?
Normality is just a word
Not one speck is normal,
Each different in all respects
From Edinburgh to Cornwall,
Dependent upon your mind
Your deduction and philosophy,
How you find the world at large
Gives an answer, decidedly.
On the one hand 'tis profound
Specie and sub-specie, intelligence,
On the other, banal and cruel
Defining such crude intent.
Fighting and cruelty still rife
I believe it's profound we're still here,
Normality then combines the two,
Beguiling, is the rarest, I fear.

Everyday
an
Overview

Everyone in every house
Give or take an hour or two,
Back from school and work on time,
This is, of course, an overview.

Buttons are pressed for a TV night,
For the hour stands at 6 o'clock,
After washing hands and change of shoes
It's time for tea, either cold or hot.

Now for gossip of the day,
Evening papers scanned,
A last few moments for children's play
Adults think some music, should be banned.

Offspring in bed now asleep
Parents settle to the play,
An hour or so before retiring
Then to sleep and another day.

Beyond the Sky

And when the spaceships,
    Start to fly
To those bright stars
    Beyond the sky –

Carrying the spirits
    Of courageous men,
On tails of fire
    To heaven sent.

Theirs to uncover
    The treasure of gods,
And acceptance
    Of those who trod –

The path of knowledge
    As others, too,
Throughout ages
    To this point grew.

And held dominion
    In their time,
So to Earthmen
    Their rise will shine.

Why Green?

Why is a greenhouse called green?
Not red, yellow or blue,
    Which is, the right colour?
    Just what is, the right hue?

Green, they say, is the obvious choice
A nursery where plant seeds grew
    And all plants are green, except
    Flowers, which are red, yellow and blue.

So, why is a greenhouse called green?
When plants have so many colours,
    Green is so very universal
    The colour, that dominates all others.

Each Life a Witness

Each life, a witness to
This uncontrolled, unscripted
Gamble, of one's self. Born
Amidst this turmoil. Conscripted
Into this ant-like colony
Of concrete and brick with highways
That emulate columns of insects
     As each behind the other, cars stay –

In procession, ant-like
Each day, enough to turn the mind,
And rules and laws abound
Such, as to restrict life and confine.
Notwithstanding control freaks
Interfering, and politically
Correct police targeting the wrong
     People, unjustifiably

Then of course, there's terrorists
Just to add to the charm,
Who seem to rule where they exist,
Spreading terror and alarm.
As time moves constantly on
Humanity regresses in part,
Belief in force over wisdom
     Holds back the spirit and heart.

Rhythmic Recollection

Where is the locomotive?
That driven head of steam.
Powering the eight-coach train
Thundering on steel, supreme.

Each blast of the whistle
Sent a warning down the line
And to stand on a platform
When she roared on through, sublime.

The rhythmic beat of power
Through piston, crank and wheel,
Pulsed upon the very air
Heard in valley, town and weald.

Smoke and steam from funnel streaming
Down the years she laboured,
Carrying the nation's history
Once for travel, favoured.

Now in twilight, passes,
Her rhythmic song grows faint,
Into the darkness the glow,
Of the red rear lamp, slowly fades.

Far Too Many, Far Too Few

The earth is only so big
The planet is finite in size,
Two-thirds of it is water
It's limited in area and supplies,
Yet the human race uncaring
Keeps on reproducing and growing,
With no thought of dwindling land
> As if they were totally unknowing.

Unless we make provision
Laws and plans to counteract
This explosive situation,
> And we have not long to act –

For on the one hand we have too many
And on the other far too few,
Unless the cold lands and the deserts
Can be revived and used –
I see the darkest trouble
Brewing on the horizon.
Trouble not easily overcome
> As a warning shadow rises on –

> Humanity and earth to come.

So Short a Span

Dragonflies of green and blue
    Damselflies colourful too.

Butterflies of many a hue
    Through summer bright and new,

Autumn shows only a few
    They are born to die too soon,

As if these creatures knew
    Their life, so short a span drew,

Took each hour, each day due
    Lived, and onwards exotically flew.

A Play on Humorous Strife

Cat meowing at a mouse
Dog barking at the cat,
Man shouting at the dog
Wife scolding the man.

Mouse, cat, dog, man and wife
All adding to the noise,
Each the other cursing
With each strident voice.

'Til the cat chased the mouse
The dog lay down to sleep,
The man went back to work
Wife, her house to keep.

All the while, cat and mouse,
Dog dreaming of the cat,
Man mumbling to himself,
Wife grumpily sat.

'Tis just a play on everyday strife
'Twixt mouse, cat, dog, man and wife.

By Circle and Spoke

Within the city a thousand shops
A thousand homes and apartment blocks,
Here and there a green-space park
With wrought-iron ornamental clock.

A fast-lane'd bypass circles round
While many roads like spokes are found,
Radiating to the centre
Guiding traffic city bound.

Diverse traffic lights and road signs,
Pedestrian crossings show it's time,
To cross each busy highway
Before 'GO' is flashed in green, bright shines.

Literature held in libraries
Theatres producing plays, nightly,
Cinemas, hotels and restaurants
Advertise relaxation full brightly.

The airport and railway station
Offer escape and way to hasten,
Your passage to and from the city
Or by car, on roads like spokes, on occasion.

Soft Autumn Light

In butter-colour softness
    The autumn light of morning,
Washes over the countryside
    A muted golden awning.
A morning of tranquillity
    As quietly, the lightest breeze,
Brushed the low hedgerows
    Gently shaking the changing trees –

Whose leaves had turned to match
    The risen sun in colour,
Along with the yellows
    Of dried grass and straw of summer,
White heads of mushrooms appear
    Above the ground in meadows,
And at the foot of shrub and tree
    Falls the fruit of summer, grown.

A flash of fur on hurried feet
    The squirrel scampers with his find,
Hoarding seeds and nuts for winter
    Amongst the woodland and the pines.
Slowly the day moves on
    To insects' lazy drone of song,
Until the mists of evening fall
    To twilight, then, the day is gone.

Unwittingly Tied

The insanity of a large part
    Of earth's restless humanity,
Has been fuelled by ancient beliefs
    Continued indoctrination and banality.

A trap set many aeons ago
    By ancient command decreed,
Man was steered unto this unenlightened
    Void of belief and disbelief of deed –

So on and onward throughout history
    Man was tied and never free,
To understand the world around him
    The choice was made and unwittingly –

Was led by doctrine and fanatical fervour
    Ever deeper, ever more unknowing,
So obligingly into the trap did he fall
    He may never have seen true light growing.

Yet his very mind, overcame the false
    And aware of knowledge making clear,
Sought for wisdom and put away the fears
    To find the truth of man and his early years.

Many a Spirit

The weather-worn tables and benches
 Still standing in the garden
 Of the country village inn,
 Denied the season being autumn.

Autumnal coloured leaves dropped
 From bordering trees to carpet
 In gold, russet and brown, the ground
 Beneath the visiting footsteps.

Then tabletops and garden all
 Were bathed in tranquil sunlight,
 That lit the countryside just as
 A giant stage-setting might.

Many a year the inn has stood
 And many an autumn had seen,
 A spirit of warmth and welcome
 Pervaded the setting and did seem –

This spot, unchanged over the years
 This very place for drink and merriment,
 Held the spirit, the enchantment
 Of laughter and many a jibe well meant,

  For many a spirit who came and went.

A Waiting Rose

A late rose of October
    Moved constantly in the wind,
The pink-white petalled face
    A small beacon in the garden trim.

One or two late buds also
    Reluctant to show their graces,
Held closed their spirit of form
    'Til sunlight warmed their faces.

As each day progresses at this time
    The grey of approaching cold weather
Continues to define,
    The cooling air from autumn's whisper –

Of summer's end betwixt and winter,
    Yet the rose clings on still awhile,
Awaiting a late sunbeam's smile
    To show her face and perhaps beguile.

Nearer the Clouds

When true love comes at last
Embracing her and him,
    Each, such feelings for the other
    Love exceeding exotic sin.

To kiss, pet and fondle,
Hands so securely clasped,
    Eyes a-twinkle with happiness
    For love that will last and last.

When, not of this world's reality
Two minds are nearer the clouds,
    It is as if far heaven
    Has lifted them from the ground –

And placed them in a faerie tale
A new land of enchantment,
    Where life will be forever
    For them, a starlit apartment.

Denoting the Difference

Have you noticed this one thing
    No matter what it is or be
    About life, the world and everything,
    There is one difference we can see?
This pertains to all there is
    Every aspect of what we are,
    What we do, eat, write, sing or make
    From a bicycle to a car.
The very word itself explains
    The meaning of 'Good' in praise,
    Example, 'that's good, that's better,
    Head and shoulders above', terms we lay
On diverse objects, art, writing,
    Songs, clothes etc., throughout humanity
    A word that separates a few from others
    Denoting a difference of quality.
For 'Good' stands above the bland,
    Above the mediocre depicting the need
    To own such quality, even to necessity,
    Or strive for 'Good', or be the best, to lead.

Nothing and All

Clock tickety clock
The time has gone,
The time has run
    Yet time runs on.

Ticking clock and silent
Measure length of day,
And also every night
    Continue to obey.

What is being measured?
What is this time?
Uncounted by number
    Unread by ruler line.

Passing time cannot
Be, by us measured,
Whether hour, day, month or year
    Time cannot be fettered.

For it's nothing and all,
The unbound movement
Of everything that exists,
    Moving, changing, slowly meant,

    The universe augments.

Blows the Wind

Wind in the tall elms
And the silver birches,
Rustling the willows
Stirring the larches.

Blows the wind freely
Round the chimney pots,
Past the high gables
Over the rooftops.

Moving the hedgerows
Bordering the gardens,
Sweeping the meadows
Valley, hill and fen.

Leaves made to dance,
To swirl round and round,
Wind, a sign of change,
To winter, we are bound.

Yesterday

I remember yesterday
When the world was almost sane,
Beginning sixty years ago
Fifteen years old, and life was a game.
Through the years I've noticed
The subtleties and changes
That slowly turned the innocent
     Immoral, turning history's pages –

To gratify New Age leaders
And their liberal scepticism,
Half-thought-out party ideas
     Of honour, truth and patriotism.

Into the future we may be moving
That does not mean we need complexity,
Or party dogma to restrict our lives,
Whatever happened to simplicity?
A way of life once revered
Now scorned by political jobsworths,
Who do not understand that freedom
     Has been dearly bought and so must conserve.

Too many government laws
Far too many restrictive rules,
People cannot live like that
Do they really think we are fools?
Whatever happened to yesterday
Of living without the lies,
For God's sake stop this stupidity
     And return to a British way of life.

The Very People

With pressure and fear,
    Intimidations to involve,
The EU persistently attacks
    The British nation, to control.

The very people, the country
    That went to war, to help
These European nations
    Fight aggression, for it was felt –

It was our duty so to do,
    And so this small island stood firm,
And fought the aggressive foe,
    Outnumbered, and outgunned, did learn –

The mighty challenge she took on
    Yet never wavered in her duty,
Took on the enemy wherever
    He was found, and thus refuted –

The enemy's claim of masterful
    Lords, controlling the earth,
Helping to subjugate the foe
    Restoring living humanity first.

Thus the war did finally end,
    Those nations helped by Great Britain
Should acknowledge this sacrifice
    And remove the directive, written.

For, Great Britain is not part of Europe
    She is set aside from the mainland,
As was shown in the past
    She is not to be controlled, this England!

The Ladder of the Mind

When time for earth runs out,
And the world is old,
Who will tell the story
When all that was, is cold?

Who will tell the history
Of this planet's peoples,
The wars and conquests
Striving to seek all?

Failures and successes,
Set back a thousand times,
Yet slowly did ascend
The ladder of the mind.

Who will know the outcome?
Will mankind find his place?
Will he obtain the knowledge
To fly in cosmic space?

Or fall from attempted grace
To languish, race and gender,
Upon this aging sphere
To slowly die, trapped forever.

Temperature, Humidity and Time

Temperature, humidity and Time
Instrumentation we live by,
Each offering information
   For us, in our lives to apply.

Each individual instrument
Gives an accurate reading,
Temperature, hot, warm, cold, freezing
   If hot, cold drinks, if, cold, then sneezing.

Humidity, makes one perspire
If too much water vapour's in the air,
Feels like walking through soup
   Takes one's energy, nothing can compare.

Then of course, we come to old time
Recording the hours day and night,
Telling us hurry, smile, work completed,
   This is the instrument always in sight.

Yet, I wonder at this situation,
Are these instruments our servants,
Which we continuously rely on
   Or are **we** servants of these instruments?

On Lake, River and Sea

A boat on the river
In the warmth of the summer,
    Is so laid-back and cool
        And relaxing in manner.

It could be a dinghy
With youngsters aboard,
    A tall-masted yacht
        On river or broad.

Or a motor cruiser
For the family,
    With drinks on the aft deck
        Dinner in the galley.

The roar of a speedboat
In the estuary,
    Bow high as she speeds
        Into a westerly.

Yet again, for quiet
A fishing boat at sea,
    Rowing boat on lake
        Or country river scene.

Colourful Shades and Shadows

Apricot skies
  Over green lemon fields,

Deep plum are the shadows
  By liquorice weald.

Candy-coloured evenings
  With sun-orange glow –

As it rests on the distant
  Damson cloud pillow –

That lays on horizons
  Ripe fruit of the grapevine –

Awaiting the blackberry
  Of night dark rich wine.

Hundreds of thousands
  Starlit are soon –

Sprinkled over all,
  Above a sugar-ice moon.

White

White candlesticks
White candles
And
White Kendal mint cake.

White chicken breast
White crusty bread
And
Ovens full of bake.

White sugared pies
White vintage wine
And
White greeting cards.

White hanging balls
White bearded father
And
White flashing stars.

Mingling with lamps
Red, green and blue
And
Treetop faeries.

Just waiting for frost
And cold winter snow
And
Then we'll be merry,

And
Put on a show!

Both of These

Is it mind or muscle
That forges the way ahead?
    Is it the mental tussle
    Or strength of arm and leg?

It could be said of strongmen
Who weald the maker's tools,
    They it is who build and mould
    And strength, not weakness rules.

Yet nothing can be done
Without the mind to fathom,
    It takes great intellect
    Creating and to fashion.

Thus it falls to both of these,
For strength of arm we need,
    To construct and manufacture
    What the clever mind foresees.

Created in the Mind

There is a hidden danger
A mask'd unseen device,
Unknown to most of us
Yet through all history lies,
Unseen, unfelt, unwanted,
Dormant it lies in some,
Others it is activated
  Becomes most troublesome.

Long ago this thought-like probe
Was created in the mind,
Awaiting each favoured chance
To disrupt human kind.
For working deep within
Humanity's flawed design,
Is a pathological weapon
  A secret hidden mine.

Expansion to Contraction

Through and beyond the deepest black,
  Beyond the Magellanic Clouds,
  Further than existing time
  And colliding galactic shrouds –

To the point of no return
  For out of depth and out of mind,
  Beyond the oldest remnant shine
  There is no existence to confine –

There is just before time
  Until the point of conflagration,
  Where the stretch and pull of gravity
  Reaches the point of disintegration –

Returning great and small once more
  To particles of gas and dust,
  Reversing expansion to contraction
  Pulling all back as it must –

Compressing all, once again
  Possibly to the point of compression,
  With uncontrolled ignition
  Explosion and expansion.

When the Stars Wove Patterns New
A Work of Fantasy

There was a time it has been said
  Long before mankind was born,
  A period of strange ability,
  After days of reptile and dragon
  When the moon circled closer,
  Over the tower of complexity –

When the sun shone blue on morning dew
  And the stars wove patterns new,
  Bright comets seared across the sky,
  Lighting up clouds like hanging lamps
  Hung upon a ceiling high,
  Which on the winds did fleeting fly –

Across the land and mountain dark
  Where the deep and brooding woods
  Did mark the place for elvish folk,
  Wolf, bear, and many a strange lair
  Together did abide there,
  Amongst the trees and great arm'd oak –

Which stood at the very heart
  Of the great fearful wildwood
  The living heart, unseen, remote,
  In shadowed mystery,
  Where spiteful goblins lived
  To trick, then vanish in the undergrowth.

And all the while the tall grey tower
  Upon the mountain plateau,
  Stood stark and menacing,
  Against the sunset light
  That caught the many high-blown flakes
  Of cloud in a red-gold confection –

That swept the sky as a coverlet
    Beckoning the darkening sky to sleep,
    To sleep but for a moment before,
    A brilliance of purple flame arose
    Like a living cloak spreading on high
    From the tower with an unearthly roar –

And spitting sparks of red and green
    That climbed into the twilight sky
    Followed by more and more,
    It must have been the strangest sight
    To see gold, purple, red and green
    In flame and spark, meet in magicians' lore.

Thus dims the light, as night befalls
    And falling stars as meteors
    Criss-cross the powdered heavens high,
    Like messengers to the gods
    Or faerie cosmic cars a-glowing,
    Through the very spaces fly.

While ribbon light snakes on the ground
    Is it alive or just light profound,
    That lights the eyes of many strange crea-
tures
    Weird are these small animals
    Who climb and jump and bite, for,
    They have pointed teeth and ugly features.

Suddenly all is lit in silver light
    The moon, ten times its size today
    Has risen from the horizon
    Majestic, gigantic, unshaded face
    Overwhelms the layered night
    As an enormous balloon arising –

Hanging, staring down, shining
   With reflected light
   Threatening in its magnitude,
   While pulsating true mystery
   Is in the air and everywhere
   An energy in everything imbued.

And it was said by ancient ones
   This time of mystery was found
   Before the time of men and after reptiles ran,
   When the moon rode so much closer,
   And where not man, yet someone else
   With power of magic did understand.

So, dear reader, if you have read
   This poetic tale from beginning to end,
   Does it strike you as impossible,
   That such strange times are feasible?
   Or do you think they are nonsense?
   Just images from a poet's stall –

OR

   Is there in your subconscious
   A tiny spark, perhaps, or wish,
   To really know why such tales enthral?

Timeless Testimony

He was one of a kind,
In his mind he walked alone,
By the hedgerows' dusty track
 Over the hills where stood the stone –

Thence 'cross the plain to standing trees
For with memory dim as yet,
And clouded, did show where once
 The old village long ago was set.

And in his mind the thunder
Of horses' hooves did sound,
Along the beaten earthy road
 Hidden now beneath the ground.

Still in his search for memory,
Upon the shifting breeze did hear,
The mystic sound of ancient pipes
 Recalling old music to the ear.

As round about him, now, he heard
Laughter of children and guttural speech,
And smelt the wood-fire smoke and aroma
 Of spit-turned roasting meat.

Shades, shadows or spirits,
He could not tell where reality
And imagination merged
 Or whether it be a dream.

His spirit seemed to be elsewhere
Yet as he alone, stood there,
Drifting in and out of time
    He knew he had once lived here.

A soul out of time perhaps
Or did his very being retain,
Images of days long gone
    Of past life lived again.

Was he one of a kind?
Perhaps he was not alone,
And did the deeds of lives
    Long past, remain like the stone? –

To haunt us in our future days
And take us back in memory,
To faraway times once known
    In continuous timeless testimony.

Of Red and Softest Green

He swept down fast from shadowed tree
    To land upon the fresh-cut grass,
And looked about expectantly,
    Until satisfied at last –

He strode beneath a weeping birch
    To find some morsel hidden there,
A handsome bird of green and red
    Striking of presence and rare.

Strutting among the hanging fronds
    Finding breakfast for a moment,
Then satisfied he'd garnered all
    On green wing, to air and sky went.

A flash of red and softest green
    Was far too soon lost to sight,
But you could hear him in the trees
    Tapping the wood with all his might.

The Prize

Whenever you see it sailing high
The moon, for all its story
Is airless, dead, un-alluring,
Has no power, has no glory.
Its light comes from the sun
Reflected off its surface,
As it catches the sun's rays
    From beyond night-dark space.

Yet the moon has more to offer
With its fascinating phases,
And features romantically
    In poetic verse and lovers' phrases.

And bequeaths us more to view
As she circles close and then,
Drifts further away, higher, brighter,
Returning slowly to once more send –
Her golden harvest orb arising
Majestically into the night above,
To hang as a lover's lamp
    And that's the prize, the moon we love.

A Symbol

A white butterfly on a red rose
    A picture of such clarity,
In the last of autumn's warmth
    Lit by the sun's distant disparity –

From summer's hot bright days
    As the seasons fast become winter,
Yet, but for a passing space of time
    A butterfly white of hue did partner –

A single red rose that bloomed,
    The last upon the bush to grow,
And for one brief moment
    Caught in the softening glow –

That fell upon the garden
    Shone forth a sign of purity,
Of life and blood, a symbol
    For all that's good in nature's beauty.

Early 'Til Late

The roads in the country
Are so busy at harvest,
And into the autumn
For there is no rest –

For tractor and trailer
And open-back truck,
Ferrying the produce
To the wholesalers' huts.

From early 'til late
Each day by the load,
Are carried by crate
Or weight, and bestowed –

On produce dispatchers
Who collect and clean,
Pick and select
From a swede to a bean.

Potatoes, onions, carrots,
Cabbage, peas and beetroot,
More from apple orchards
Pear, plum and soft fruits.

Back and forth they go
Each wagon full, again,
Transported throughout the land
In packing station's name.

Fruit, veg and grain for bread
Wheat, barley, oats and maize,
All by road from farm must go
To feed us all, for days and days.

Water

This may not commonly be known
    By ordinary folk who doubt,
And shall we say 'tis not widely
    Or broadly talked about.
And come what may none will alter
    The very fact that fresh water
Is the daughter of the sea
    And returns as if by halter,
In a cycle with the weather,
    And is brought to us in clouds,
Which are made by heat and cold
    In evaporated vapour bound,
To fall again once more as rain,
    To fill the rivers, lakes and springs,
Soak the earth to feed the grain
    And give to all the life it brings.

Within a Morphean Cloud

To rest upon bright golden clouds
Seen within the mind-wrought dream,
By those in enchanted sleep
　　Are enfolded now, perchance to seek,
Unknown realms which in the mind
Can excite, or open up reality,
Distanced from actuality
　　Yet through such dreaming can free
The mind within the Morphean cloud,
From common tribulations,
Replacing strength and ill health
　　When the mind travels exotic locations.
Perhaps a journey learned and profound
Offering answers subconsciously asked,
Then again, such cloud-bestowed rest
　　Is the gold-bound sleep of the just –

　　And all that lies beyond, is masked.

A Treaty Irrespective

Thus it seems Britain has capitulated
To the Brussels non-elect,
And the EU directives regardless
Of the fact, the British could not object
To this agreement, by the very fact
That after agreeing to a referendum,
And then reneging upon this statement
Took away the British right of decision.

It does not matter who or how many
Countries sign the Agreement Directive,
If the British were not asked, or
Given any choice, then by elected
Rules, there is no binding in English law,
The federal bureaucrats' bullying scheme
Will not work in Great Britain,
They've tried that, as history has seen –

Which ended in failure thrice tried,
Now they believe they have us cornered,
But in the end, the English will,
However long it takes, remove the torment,
Which under the guise of federal manipulation
To prevent individual countries from war,
And bind all together in friendship,
Yet, this idea of friendship is to rule –

With vigour more and more!
And Britain will end up as a state
Of a non-elected whore!

Lifestyle

If your lifestyle appears bereft
    Of joy and happiness,
    Then make a choice between
    What you have or a quest,
    Beyond the present to
    A distant unknown realm,
    Where happiness is more at hand
    And a change of lifestyle could quell –

This shallow living felt
    By perhaps a life resented,
    Because you have not achieved
    That, which you really intended.
    Despondency and anger
    Are part of human emotion,
    Most of us have these feelings
    Now and again, yet remain unspoken.

You have the will and free choice
    No one is chained to a life,
    Providing you do not hurt another
    Move forward with new ideas to right,
    The problem, for only you can change
    Your state of mind and style,
    And unless you try, nothing else
    Will make you upwardly mobile.

As a Balm

To sleep, to sleep and rest
The mind and body,
　　After the wearisome day
　　To wake clear in thought, ready –

For the new day's twists and turns
And problems new to solve,
　　No matter the trade or profession
　　Life presents such tricks to resolve.

Hectic hours and days with thoughts
Of personality and love,
　　Fame or money worries
　　We all have, over and above.

Therein lies the problem
To clear the mind, rest the body,
　　Remove all worries each day
　　Not by mistakes become sorry.

We need to sleep, to sleep
The deep sleep of Morpheus,
　　Then as a balm to heal
　　Remove life's weariness.

Thingamabobs

Doodahs, whatsits and thingamagigs
    Names that are given sometimes,
To pieces of machinery
    Gadgets like thingamabobs we find.

Wartime work brought out the nonsense
    For comic names were justified,
In every case by those who handled
    Complicated machines, for it implied –

It made a most important object
    That was needed in plane, tank or gun,
Or secret things for secret agents
    Nobody knew what was made or done –

For at the time one did not speak
    Or mention what was made,
Because of spies, and the Ministry
    Of War told all, they must obey –

To keep silent on everything
    To do with war production jobs,
So all that was manufactured
    Were known as Thingamabobs.

Clear of Eye
Part One of a Dilogy

Young in mind and body
And clear of eye,

Young of heart and thought
Under a clear blue sky,

Such clarity of youth
In self and in belief,

Facing the future
Undaunted to feed –

The growing ache for knowledge,
Or to take a part –

In some worldly event,
For perhaps the start –

Of becoming a leading star
On the world's great stage,

Such clearness of vision
Wrought by youthful days.

Yet, so little a time
Has youth, when clear of eye,

To be young in heart and thought
Under a clear blue sky.

Misty of Eye
Part Two of a Dilogy

Mature in mind and body
And misty of eye,

Still young in heart and thought
Under a grey-cast sky.

Experience with age
Knows self and the years,

Living the past teaches
Understanding and fears.

The ache for what once was
When one took part and more –

In some worldly event
Or helped to stop a war.

The love of family
Brought up to be aware –

Of what they have achieved
With parental help to share.

Yet, so little a time
Has age, when misty of eye,

To remain young in heart and thought
Under a grey-cast sky.

A Hydrous Blanket

Such a dampening mist
That shares the autumn air,
    As the year approaches winter
    A shroud of grey everywhere –

Like an opaque cloud
Hanging quietly suspended,
    Uncounted microdots
    Of water vapour, blended.

An airborne coverlet
As a hydrous blanket,
    Lies low, obscuring day
    Until with warmth is met.

Then 'tis but a moment
For the sun's rays to penetrate
    And disperse this laying cloak,
    Then sight and day, once more relate.

When the World Was Young

A long time ago
When the world was young,
Where skies of clearest blue
    Like a topaz coverlet hung –

Above the emerald fields
Woodland and river flow,
On a world that basked
    Beneath a golden glow –

That lit the white-topped mountains
In a blaze of tinted crystal,
Upon the jetted black and grey
    Of the upward-thrusting rock wall.

And reflected from lapis lazuli
Sparkling seas, that rolled
Towards far-distant shores,
    Glistening like speckled gold.

While upon the verdant plains
Ran the animals sure and free,
Before the mind of man
    Destined him to intercede.

Serenity

Within this world of wild chaos
    Fraught with war and ignorance,
Where noise is found everywhere
    And you are treated with indifference,

What a paradise then to find
    A haven quiet and serene,
Such a place of tranquillity
    As heaven sent would seem.

Yet, to have lived in the city
    And in the countryside,
Knowing both for what they are
    Thus whatever is implied –

The city has expanded
    Taking over rural pastures,
Felling trees and mighty forests
    A spreading concrete disaster –

Leaving fewer and fewer
    Acres of natural countryside,
Quaint villages, streams, waterfalls
    Where our native birds can fly.

Or we as spiritual beings
    Can obtain that restful calm,
That restores the mind and body
    A relaxing natural balm.

For those who seek yet, the peace
    Of rural England, to obtain
That elusive serenity that haunts
    The spirit, is not in vain –

Like the golden chalice lost,
    One must seek for such dreams,
They lie, still to be discovered
    Amongst the hills, dells, wheat and bean.

The picture in your mind's eye
    If you have the sincerity,
Is still to be achieved
    If you really wish for serenity.

Gentle and with Grace

If you think the lady fair
  To be gentle and with grace,
    As told in tales of old
      And all fair of face –

Were not like those today
  Whose outward looks deceive,
    As some are good to look upon
      Others, more a man to perceive.

The female may be fair
  But, gentle and with grace?
    I think not, for she has
      A claw-like temperament laced –

With a spiteful temper
  Equal to a man's rage,
    And yet more subtle, designed
      To catch no matter the age –

Such prey, unwittingly unaware,
  Yet, there are those, fair and of grace,
    Gentle and feminine, who care
      As there are still gentlemen of taste.

The Gold Leaves of Autumn

The gold leaves of autumn
Are the memories of summer,
From the bright burning sun
To dandelions and clover.

The gold of the cornfields
And yellow of the hay,
Carpets of buttercups
Over meadows, fresh lay.

When sweet-scented roses
Perfumed the warm air,
With blossoms of shrubs, pendants
Of gold, laburnums bear –

Russet of apple, yellow of pear,
Apricot and peach all hold,
The colours that are seen
In autumn leaves of gold.

To Higher Planes

Beware the sun's hot temperament
Strongly fierce and independent,
When upon those languid moments
Your mind to life's secrets is bent –

For knowledge you are seeking
And answers to be found,
Questions that lie beyond
The spirit's ability and confound.

Better, thoughts are freed at time
Of moonlight drifting over cloud,
Casting soft-moving shadows
That cloak such thoughts bound –

To higher planes of existence
Above the earth in spatial dark,
Dimensional path concealed
Or riding the winds to hark –

Listening with an inner heart
Yet of a spirit open to thought,
For secrets are there to be sought
If from a mind that can be caught.

To Slumber Long and Still

To sleep below within the ground
Or up above the billowed clouds,
To rest and sleep the sleep of time
    Enfolded in silent hours.

To think no thoughts or listen
And speak no words good or ill,
Just to rest the aching body
    The mind to slumber long and still.

Whatever time did pass on earth
Whatever age did come and go,
In my sleep I'll not awaken
    'Til the time of rebirth know.

Perception

When we were young it seemed
The seasons did come and go,
Yet each was as a year
And each year a lifetime slow.

So young in age and mind
Primed with energy all day,
All around an adventure ground
Whilst we were at our play.

Shouting, running, laughing
Activities without number,
Then almost falling asleep
Before bedtime and slumber.

How perception has changed
Now that we are adult,
The seasons quickly pass
And the year like a season bolts.

Now I wish for each season
A year and each year a lifetime
Could be, for us whose lives rush on
As the passing years remind.

Just a Picture

I remember summers
And days of a long time ago,
Such long days, warm and bright
So much to do, places to go.

Picnics in the country
By a meadow, woodland and stream,
We set the kettle to boil
And waited for the hiss of steam.

With our backs against a log
And a cloth spread out before us,
The plates of sandwiches
Covered to keep off the dust.

Cheese 'n' tomato, fish paste
And cucumber made such a feast,
With a bag of Smith's crisps
Lemonade or a cup of tea.

In shade from woodland trees
And the sound of running brook,
That now in memory
Is just a picture in life's book.

The Lamp

The oil lamp stands unused
    Just an ornament that sits,
A relic from a bygone age
    Of such differences –

When it lit a world so sure
    Of itself, themselves and duty,
Divided into classes
    Each in their place suited.

When the lamp was cleaned
    And perfectly polished,
With all objets d'art in the house
    By servants, if not, were admonished.

When evening closed in
    Velvet drapes were drawn,
The lamp was lit to accompany
    Light from the flickering fire's warmth.

The sound of traffic, horses' hooves
    And iron tyres of a carriage,
Comes softly from the street
    As he and she, still stiff in marriage –

    Observed propriety's conceit.

By Legislation, Chain the Free

Thus, we pay for history
    Of foreign armies and destruction,
Made to pay for misery
    Caused by wars and corruption.
Each succeeding generation
    Is made aware of tragedy,
By taxes and ill-prepared laws
    That make of freedom a travesty.
To generate a superstate
    Each country tied by agreed
Directives, that will stifle
    By legislation and chain the free.

All brought about by false guise
    Of denying countries the ability
To start wars, but in actuality
    Accomplishes all, that war's finality
Brings about, the domination
    Of people, nations, dreams and hopes
By those enthused to carry out
    And rule this superstate, without vote
Or with agreement by our nation
    That disregards and disrespects,
All that in history we have achieved
    For this undisguised undemocratic concept.

Stew

When draughts and cold winter winds
    Begin to blow around the house,
Or cottage small in country set
    Down lane or track by garden bower.

When trees are devoid of leaves
    Where not a single bloom or flower
Remains to remind of summer,
    And the rain is a constant shower.

How comforting to smell the stew
    That upon the hob is heating,
Potatoes, carrots, parsnips and onions
    Accompanied by gravy and steak full lean.

Fresh bread rolls waiting by the side
    To be split and spread with fresh butter,
A side accompaniment
    To this English dinner or supper.

When the cold winds of winter
    Occupy the world outside,
Think how cosy you can be
    With the feast, mouth-watering stew provides.

This Secular World of Winter

In our secular world of winter
 With mud, puddles and wet leaves,
Bare-branched trees outlined by light
 And pale-yellow yolk of sun, which flees –

So quickly across the watery sky
 From dawn to red-dyed dusk,
Gives but so few in hours of day
 Accompanied by winds' strong gusts –

Which coldly blow across fallow field
 Crop and meadow, farm and town,
Bearing cloud and rain once more to soak
 The already waterlogged ground.

Where horses huddle by hedgerow's lee
 The woodlands smell of musk and mould,
Pheasant and partridge scarce are found
 And the rivers run deep and cold.

Yet upon horizon's line
 Christmas approaches with such glitter,
To raise the spirits of all once more
 In this secular world of winter.

The Last Soldier

*H*is breath came in gasps as he ran
Forward toward the enemy,
Missiles and lances of light tore past,
     Explosives erupted ahead as he –

Heard the hoarse shouted order given
And he dropped behind a ruined wall,
The noise of fighting continued
     Around him, as he waited for the call –

The command to advance once more
Yet no command came, no order to advance,
So he stayed behind the broken wall
     Half awake, half asleep as in a trance.

He finally awoke from a fitful sleep
Stiff, haggard and aching, to find
An early sun shining low in the sky,
     Dew lay upon the ground and himself, why –

Wasn't he dead? That last push forward
Had cost the brigade dear, so many
Causalities, what was wrong? This silence?
     His mind was confused, where was the enemy?

He lay there, his back against the wall
How long he lay he did not know,
Slowly he stood and surveyed the scene
     Only ruins and bodies, he was alone.

The stench of munitions hung in the air
As his mind took in all that he saw,
He made his way through the rubble
     Stumbling and cursing the futile war.

None did he see, as he moved amongst
The burnt-out buildings, vehicles and bones,
Skeletal remains of powerful armies
     Who fought a war where none came home.

Finally, he came across a fountain
Where water still flowed afresh,
And on the surrounding parapet
    Sat a child, a girl in a torn dress.

He bid her good-day as well as he could
And sat on the wall beside her,
Dusty of face and dirty of hands
    She stared into the water.

He took her hand and gently asked
Her name and where she lived
Slowly she turned and looked at him
    "Are you the father I should be with?"

The soldier looked at her with pity
"No," he replied, "I'm just a friend."
"I don't know where everyone's gone,"
    The young girl said. "Are they going to send –

People to clean up this mess?"
"Oh, I expect so," replied the soldier,
And taking hold of her hand
    Stood, for it had become much colder.

And he must seek shelter for now
He had the responsibility
Of a young life in his hands,
    He must keep her safe and show civility.

At last by a small kindling fire
She asked him to hold her,
"Are you someone special?" she whispered.
    He smiled. "No, perhaps, just the last soldier."

A Poet's Lot

A poet's lot is an estranged lot
    Part of, amongst, yet distant
From mainstream life and everyday things,
    But more conscious of life and the instant,
In a spiritual way of understanding
    That compels the writer to compose
Through emotional or natural
    Genuine empathy, his verse or prose.
As there are those in professions
    Of learning, expertise that exists
In trades that befit their abilities,
    So the poet should be acknowledged in his.

Out of Step, Out of Time

'Tis such a pity that our world
We all knew as children,
Through youth to young adult
    Quickly passes unbidden.

Yet, still passes so slowly
We do not realise the times
Are changing, for we are part of it all,
    Until one day it's brought to mind –

That life has changed and we are older,
The world is a different place,
And we are slightly out of step
    Out of time and out of phase.

We did not see the subtle change
Occurring day by day compounding,
'Til the years gathered them all,
    Rushing into the future, crowding –

And concertinaing the days
Until suddenly aware,
We have changed, no longer young
    In a world now so *contraire*.

Upon the Earth

Bright of sun
And
Bright of sky,
Bright of moon
And
Bright of eye.

Upon the earth
And
Upon the lands,
Upon nature
And
Upon the sands.

Flowing time
And
Flowing river,
Flowing thoughts
And
Flowing giver

Of life.

Little Streams, Dykes and Rivers

The streams rush and bubble
The dykes fill and flow,
And the rivers rise and flood
    Their banks, as they widen and grow.

Winter's rain torrential and cold
    Day by day unremitting,
Filling every ditch and pound
    Waterlogged ground submitting –

As a sponge to soak up water
    More and more, until the land
Is saturated, a permeable reservoir
    And thus, drains to river and –

Ditch, yet further, to flood road
    And highway, track and town,
Creating chaos where such waters
    Accumulate or where found.

For little streams that rush and bubble
    And dykes that slowly grow,
Become themselves swift little rivers
    When winter rains do flow.

Changing Magnetic Poles

What if the pole of the north
Changed places with the south, or
    Swung anywhere in between
    Opposite or random to before?

Therefore, spinning compass needles
Would no longer show the north,
    But would instead point southwards
    Or anywhere to magnetic force.

Should such particle surge of flare
Penetrate metals in the ground,
    Then magnetic currents change
    And make earth's poles unsound.

'Tis not a rare phenomenon,
For poles have changed many times
    As shown in ancient rocks
    Varying magnetic lines.

But should the change be sudden
That's a different matter,
    The earth would be in turmoil
    Civilisation shattered.

Wet

Wet the sky
    Wet the air,
        Wet the ground
        Wet ev'rywhere.

Wet the hound
    Wet the cat,
        Wet is me
        Wet is fact.

Wet to see
    Wet to touch,
        Wet to show
        Wet is such –

A damp flow
    That tumbles
        Feelings low,
        Like puddles.

Wings of Time

Twenty thousand generations
Or more have flown the wings of time,
From forgotten years of long ago
    When man was young, before the climb.

Before he knew his own harsh nature
Greed, jealousy, power unborn,
When the world was young in heart
    Governed by nature's myriad forms.

For overflowing were the seas
In bountiful diverse creatures,
And fresh-wrought waves thundered
    To break upon golden, virgin beaches.

Thus, all the long ages past
With their triumphs and woes,
To the present generation
    Confirm what fleeting time shows –

Man's little understanding of place,
In life's continuum, for we as a spark,
Live for just a moment before
    We too, the wings of time must embark.

Many a Broken Word

*M*any the promises given
    Many the speeches spoken,
Many the vows proclaimed
    Many a word broken.

The lure of position
    Council or parliamentary,
Candidate, or member
    Of the House irrespectively –

Bend the truth to suit occasion
    Or omit truth altogether,
In order to make a point
    Pass a vote on party agenda.

Why can't they be true to self,
    To the people who have their trust,
Hold fast to the perception
    Or vision which they know is just? –

For the people they represent,
    To hold firm with endeavour
Until their views are acknowledged,
    And they've earned their position with honour.

Touching Sighs

The gold of flaxen hair
The sparkle in grey-green eyes.
The pouting ruby lips
The heaving breast and touching sigh –

Are all part of women's wiles
To lure the chosen man,
Beauty is to be admired
Seducing the male mind, can –

Secure her mate quite readily
Therein, such female ways
Can snare her in a similar trap,
Granting him possession lays –

Open the loss of her intended
As he, drawn by another urge
Desires her but for the moment,
The bringing together and the surge –

Of passion for such a short time,
For flaxen hair, grey-green eyes,
Ruby lips and heaving breast
Can ruthlessly cause touching sighs.

This Treasury of Collected Gems

Drops of rain like jewels,
Glistening liquid crystal,
Or as sparkling diamonds
From passing clouds do fall.

From summer shower to autumn
Brilliant gems thread their way,
Through air from high above
Each drop to feed the land, for May –

Time buds and blossoms once more
To show the beauty of spring,
And fill each lake and river
With a freshness only raindrops bring.

And when the days are hot and parched
This treasury of collected gems
Slakes the thirst of all which live,
Each liquid crystal to each blends –

To form such bodies of water
Accepting each fall to redeem
This life-giving panacea
In cavern, lake and mountain stream.

Each treasure chest of water seen.

As We Look Back

Oh what memories of youth
That race across our minds,
And come so swiftly into view
    Thoughts of those long-lost times.

Days we knew when we were young
Young in body, young in heart,
When all our future years hung
    So secure as yet not a part –

Of knowledgeable life, to be sad,
We knew not the future advent
But were happy with days we had,
    And in ourselves we were content.

Innocent and not so innocent
In our age not yet mature,
Before time taught us what life meant
    As we look back, from that future.

Between the Stars

Amid the myriad forms of life
As men, where do we stand,
    'Tis not just our earth we know
    But other worlds both small and grand.

Are we insignificant
Not ready for the great advance?
    Is our technology lacking,
    Our psychological make-up perchance –

Too primitive to become a part
Of the great confederation,
    That plies between the stars
    An ancient glorious foundation?

For surely this great order
One day this way will pass,
    And mankind must be ready
    To take his place with them at last.

Such Diverse Sounds

Sleek of body
Fleet of wing,
Trilling notes
The blackbird sings.

Starlings in trees
One to another,
Chatting excitedly
All together.

Black of feather
And coarse in noise,
The rook calls out
With his caw, caw voice.

When all the birds
Are wont to sing,
So diverse are
The sounds they bring.

Spots

Spots in the sky
    Falling through the air,
Spots on the windowpane
    Dropping everywhere.

Spots on the wallpaper
    Some on the sun,
Spots all over me
    Itchy have become.

Spots on the school books
    Desk and on the floor,
Spots from old inkwells
    In days of yore.

Spots in patterns
    For fabric and cloth,
Spots in writing
    Used as full stops.

Spots on some dogs
    As well as big cats,
Spots on fashion coats
    And on ladies' hats.

Spots are everywhere
    Both good and bad,
Spots are a creation
    Such a strange fad.

Britannia's Baker's Dozen

Millimetres to kilometres
　　Grams to kilograms,
European measurements
　　Against imperial stand.

Whatever happened to
　　Our inches and feet?
Why metres and not yards?
　　They can still compete.

Where is the good old dozen,
　　The baker's dozen so welcome,
Adding one extra, to make sure
　　The weight was worth the sum.

Coinage units in tens, not twelves
　　Britannia no longer is known,
Removed from our coins so rudely
　　An offence to the people, condoned.

Lost Years and Future Memories

As I look back I see the years
Stretching behind me like steps,
Leading up a hill, whose foot
Is lost in shifting misty depths
Of lost years and forgotten times,
Faces that come and go,
And half-remembered songs
    When the world was young to know.

But time has relentlessly run
Its course, by us so unbeknown,
As we, wrapped up in life
    Unaware the years had flown.

Now, as I turn and look
Far up the hill, the steps rise
In front of me, beckoning,
'Til lost in distance from my eyes,
Thus, I wonder at the future
Where these rising steps will take me,
To sunshine or rain, laughter or pain?
    As I tread each future memory.

Long, Short, Medium and High

Audio sonic vibrations
Travel through the air,
    Transformed into radio waves
Transmitted from here to there.
They flow around the earth
    On frequencies everywhere.

As are televised pictures
Broadcast colourful and bright,
    Photon dots transformed
Beamed and collected back to light.
Long, short, medium and high
    Ultra and very high wavelengths fight –

Side by side above and below
For each narrow bandwidth,
    Each their programme swift to reach
Viewer and listener with news and wit,
Comedy, drama or homely play
    All to inform or entertain us with.

Universal Citadel

Technological advancement
Coupled with coarseness
In a swiftly growing population
Carries an aura of falseness,
In the belief the people
Find their lives meaningful,
And so made happier
      By edicts, rules and electronic tools –

Standardising every family,
Their food, entertainment,
Travel, told what to do,
To think, by bureaucracy intent
On equalising all in life,
That all be on one level
Making each a universal
      Person, in a universal citadel.

Better to have individuality,
Freedom of choice in how to share all,
Along with spirituality
      Or deem oneself a rebel!

In Deep Winter Sun

Deep in each winter
Glitter and sparkle,
This time of the year
The Christmas marvel.

Shining bright through
The gloom and the cold,
This festive season
Is treasured like gold.

The rain, snow and dark
With ev'rything damp,
Such short days to see
And then with a lamp.

What better to uplift
The spirit of each one,
This festive Yuletide
In deep winter sun.

Such richness of fare
Ale and the wine,
Presents all waiting
This magical time,

The special dawning
Of Christmas Day,
Lights and candles
And family gay –

A garlanded tree
Tinsel and fairy
Ignoring the winter,
Momentarily.

Perfected Image

Silver hair
        And
Golden skin,
Emerald eyes
        That
Sparkling glint.

Gracious walk
        Like
No steps seen,
Lilting voice
        Made
Perfect dream.

Image this
        For
Truth or what?
Human be,
        Alien
Or robot?

County and Shire

House and home
    A cottage small,
Farm and inn
    The old town hall.

Shop and store
    Church tall steeple,
Grange or mansion
    Market people.

Park bandstand
    River wending,
By pavilion
    And gardens blending.

Town by town
    City or village,
Woodland wild
    Meadow with tillage.

Fair England's
    Beauty thus lauded,
County and shire
    Fiercely exalted.

Pen and Parchment

The pen has written,
The pages collected,
    Poem and verse
    Carefully subjected
To many a reading,
Emotion and truth
        Should not be falsely seen
        Portrayed and writ untrue.

The pen should thus write
Emotive phrases from
        Philosophical thoughts
        Feelings and observations.

Through the pen, the mind
Transfers such sight of eye,
        Feelings of anger
        Or meekness imply.
Each stroke on page helps
Verse and form relay
        Passionate love, scene of war,
        All the poet can convey –

        Pen and parchment ensure.

PART II

A DUET OF COMPLEMENTING VERSE

By

Elizabeth Stanley-Mallett

Previously published poems by the same author:
Beneath Rose-Lemon Skies – Arthur H. Stockwell Ltd, 2009
Winter Sun – Forward Press, 2009
Guiding Star – Forward Press, 2009
Before the Rainbow Fades – Arthur H. Stockwell Ltd, 2010

CONTENTS

The Puddle

The puddle languished in the lane
    Drying out in the sun,
Thunderclouds rolled overhead
And filled the hole again.

More and more rain fell down
    The puddle grew in size,
Overflowing into the road
By gusty winds, wild blown.

The storm went on for hours
    The puddle became a brook,
Spreading, growing deeper
Mowing down the flowers.

On and on it wound
    Finding out its way,
Larger now and powerful
A bubbling rushing sound.

By ditch, dyke and drain
    Tumbling and flowing,
Adding to the tumult
The puddle joins the sea again.

Silent Stones

What stories they could tell
  Those stones on Salisbury Plain,
Of times afar and peoples lost
  Of the sun worshippers' refrain.

But they are far more than that
  Far more than a token,
Of man's supplication
  And fear of the unspoken.

The silent stones stand stark
  Defying the wind and rain,
Marking the beginning of progress
  'Til the gods come back again.

A beacon to the heavens
  A calendar for time and place,
So their ships and shuttles can easily see
  Their artefacts on earth from space.

We do not have to bow the knee
  As we did in ages past,
For now we fully realise
  We are awake at last.

Not needing these false gods
  Who retarded our progress,
We do not need their presence
  Or inflicted strain and stress.

We have shown we can succeed
  And know where we belong,
We do not need the stones
  We know what's right and wrong.

Closed Minds

Closed minds shut tight on life
Miss out on learning such a lot,
There is no room for new visions
Being brainwashed, for what?

Thou shalt not laugh or smile
Jollity is a crime,
Misery, grey with meanness
Ruling all the time.

No time for enlightenment
No time for kith or kin,
Open up the bolted door
Let the sunlight in.

What is the point of bigotry?
Why be such a Bastille,
Storming the prison of life
A nicer person will unseal.

Finding reward in knowledge
Will such a pleasure be,
There is room inside the mind
For great curiosity.

Drained

Why do I feel so drained?
　　　Tired, worn out all the while,
Life has been so hard
　　　Obstacles, and no helping stile.

A fresh fight every day
　　　Frustration wears me down,
I struggle for hours on end
　　　To find a way around.

I can rarely win, each step forward
　　　Seems two steps back,
In spite of this, I struggle on
　　　Won't give up or slack.

So I am drained of energy
　　　All because I try too hard,
I need to be less pedantic
　　　Always be on guard.

A means of going slower
　　　Seek not perfection,
Accept a lesser result
　　　Dismiss all rejection.

It often takes great deal of time
　　　To find the exact setting,
Sometimes it can't be done
　　　I'm exhausted and fretting.

I wish I had more brains
　　　More patience, more skill,
The route I am taking
　　　Will only make me ill.

Did He Come to Cornwall

Some say that they believe
He, in person, came,
Accompanied by His uncle
        Of metal-merchant fame.

Joseph, a trader of renown
Dealt, traded far and wide,
And kept his precious Nephew
        Securely by his side.

The wonders of the ocean
Were expounded to Him,
Joseph landed in Cornwall
        To obtain the tin.

Amongst the delving miners
He understood their simple ways,
And promised He would return
        Again, some future day.

But it was not to be
One man scotched His plans,
His ministry was terminated
        By evil Roman hands.

Nevertheless, it may well be
He will land here again,
With timely brought knowledge
        Part of man's just claim.

This Man, this Lord may once again
Tread our ancient land,
And the splendours of the universe
        We may start to understand.

The Vet

I wanted to be an animal doctor
To use my healing hands,
To ease the aches and pains
    Of cattle, sheep and lambs.

I had no fear of animals
They responded well to me,
I could scoop up any one
    And have a good look-see.

I loved both dogs and cats
They trusted me not to harm,
Loads of money was needed
    Much more than on the farm.

My father felt the same as me
He too, yearned as a lad,
No money in the family
    Scotched any plans he had.

I can only look back and wish
I had a lot more brains,
And made a pot of money
    To enable me to train.

Animals need folk like me
People who deeply care,
Who try to improve their life
    Torn skin, broken limbs repair.

I try in my little way
To help all animals' fate,
So much more is needed
    For me it's now too late.

The Season's Cycle

Winter kisses the land with frost
And food and water is short,
The wildlife struggles to survive
Humans play with snow as sport.

Spring proffers shoots of life
Promises better fare to come,
Blossoms abound in fragrant air
Fully cherished by the sun.

Summer erupts, so hot and dry
Land is cracked and brown,
Storms redress the balance
Flooding villages and town.

Autumn's a time of plenty
Harvests of fruit and grain,
But chill in the morning air
Winter's creeping back again.

As the seasons rotate each year
Changing climate and weather,
From green spring to winter's freeze
Will they go on for ever?

Topsy-Turvy

Why are MPs called honourable?
What honour do they display?
    Who work when they feel like it
And get far too much in pay.

The world seems topsy-turvy
All the wrong way round,
    Police arresting the hero
Who brings a mugger down.

Defending property means trouble
Let the burglars roam,
    Don't attempt to stop them
Rifling through your home.

Sort your trash best you can
Watch where it goes,
    Perhaps, for once, there is a lot
And the bin overflows –

If so, it will just be left
Or you will be fined,
    Vermin breeds unchecked
Authority is so blind.

Cutting public transport
Clogs the roads with cars,
    Bring back trains, fast buses
And trams that run near and far.

Political correctness rules everywhere
Laws that make you sick,
    Why is my favourite pudding
Banned as spotted dick?

Trick or Treat

Halloween fast approaches
Time of witches riding high
Their ancient crafted broomsticks
    Silhouetted against the sky.

Time for the jack-o'-lanterns
To be lit on every shelf
Ghouls and goblins roam
    In the darkness with stealth.

'Tis a time of old custom
We call it trick or treat
Give a gift or suffer ill
    It's blackmail, rather neat.

Kids coming round, knocking doors
Are seen as unwanted pests
Nuisances demanding treats
    Showing they're scarily dressed.

Is it time to call a halt to this con?
Have we had enough
Of witches, wizards and suchlike
    Creepy frightening stuff?

Pretending to scare their elders
But to indulge in stupid pranks
In perpetrating days of old
    We have tall tales to thank.

Unlucky Thirteen

$\mathcal{H}$e tried to blow up Parliament
King James, barons, the lot,
To air the grievances of his peers
    He hatched the Gunpowder Plot.

So underneath the House
Barrels, of explosive laid,
One of his fellows had cold feet
    And the gang was betrayed.

Guy really should have known
He'd made a frightful blunder,
No way could he proceed
    Cos thirteen's an unlucky number.

Guy Fawkes was a Catholic
Who distrusted the Protestant king,
Who had stopped their work
    By banning all church building.

Fawkes was caught by King's soldiers
Apprehended in his tracks,
A traitor's death awaited him
    After torture on the rack.

He eventually disclosed all the names
Of his fellow conspirators
The King knew Guy was not alone
    Just one of many more.

November 5th is celebrated
As a great escape, is seen,
A time to be glad for the King
    Not for unlucky thirteen.

The Quiet Melody

There is a quiet melody
Enchanting, softly sensed upon the air,
It comes from unknown depths
　　And goes we know not where.

Plucking at the hardened breast,
It lingers, faint but clear,
'Til even those hearts of stone
　　Are shattered into tears.

Mystic, tune of memories past
Harmony, what might have been,
Music, soothing troubled souls
　　But avarice intervened.

Selfishness, brash noise of the many
Drowns out tranquillity,
Our melody is then subdued
　　By mean, rash stupidity.

Damaging to the ears
Jangling nerves to shreds,
Loud, crude, thumping noise
　　Fills up hospital beds.

Peace and quiet is necessary
For proper rest and respite,
The quiet melody of long ago
　　Stops such harmful blight.

When the Bond Breaks

When the bond breaks
A heart will break as well,
Life is not worth pursuing
Who is there to tell.

A woman left so much alone
Abandoned, high and dry,
Choked, broken down at last
Find the reason why.

Can it be remedied?
Can the break be mended?
Only time will reveal
What is comprehended.

Pain takes a tortured course
Leaching life from the soul,
No one can describe the rot
Or misery of this hole.

Is it worth the effort
To try to heal the breach,
Or best to leave well alone
Practise what you preach.

There are some people
Who do not dish out pain,
Time to go in the garden
Take washing out of the rain.

Of course, it's worth another go
Mending should be the aim,
Get out the sewing kit
Start living once again.

The Old Village Pub

The old pub is up for sale
Empty and left uncared,
Rooms echo the happy days
    When topers drank up there.

The cellar deep and cool
Still shows at the back,
Where barrels of the finest beer
    Were placed upon the racks.

The smell of ale still pervades
Refreshing, appetising even now,
Imbibers could sip their brew
    By the fireside's glow.

Days of happier times
When the farmer and his hand
Took a welcomed break
    From toiling on the land.

Centre of village life
A hot courier of news
Chit-chat waxed 'til "Time"
    Called an end to their views.

Who will buy the pub?
Will they like our village way?
We do not need a townie
    Who does not intend to stay.

Man with a Mission

He strode into the olde tea shop
Glowering and menacingly,
Others customers soon fled
    Leaving their cups of tea.

He was clad in black from head to foot
A page from history,
A man with a mission to fulfil
    And not to drink tea.

He had loved a lady fair
Who chose to betray him,
Taking to tumbling in the stable straw
    With handsome Ostler Jim.

Hiding back in the stable stalls
The ostler and the lass,
Saddling up two ponies fast
    Ready for a dash.

They quaked with fear
Knowing without a doubt,
That the man with a mission
    Had found their secret out.

Too late, two shots in the stable yard
One killed Ostler Jim,
The second for the vengeful man
    Who turned the gun on him.

Mortally wounded, he sank to the floor
Of the ancient coaching inn,
Now the landlord's daughter fair,
    Would neither have ostler or him.

To Grow a Soul

In this life we have the chance
To shrink into oblivion,
Or to expand our psyche
    And find our soul's horizon.

Life, at times, painfully cruel
With just a flash of blessing,
Occasionally, there it comes
    To show us what we're missing.

Knowledge garnered so laboriously
Hard-won, hard-fought and clawed,
The crowning gift for our inner heart
    Treasured, and deeply stored.

Our inner mind needs feeding
A feel-good factor requires,
Uplifting our very being
    To mingle with the higher.

This is achieved quite easily
By learning all we can,
To succour and support
    Our soul's maturing plan.

There is no end to expansion
Its growth is not finite,
Cultivated soul's have all power
    To understand and know what's right.

The Sun

The sun, orb of many moods
As it ventures on its way
Shining with blistering heat
    Turning grass into hay.

Why does this great ball of gas
Dictating of night and day
Fill all available hours
    With pleasure or dismay?

Centre of our universe
Burning, scorching in places
Source of life elsewhere
    As warmly it embraces.

From time of creation
The sun has always been
Gently coaxing produce
    To healthy fresh and green.

We cannot live without
This great monarch of the sky
Its blessings on our world
    Means we thrive or fry.

Ancient Egypt knew the sun as Ra
Prime god their writings tell
Who ruled over them dispassionately
    Instructing them as well.

So Long

It's goodbye and farewell, my love,
    You chose to play me false,
Unfaithful, a cheating skunk
I will never know the cause.

I did my best to provide for you
    Indulged your every whim,
But now my love's a total wreck
Committed to the bin.

I've really had enough
    Of being strung along,
I know you will find another
Fool like me, to hurt and wrong.

So we've split and gone our ways
    I've taken another route,
Leaving you to con your path
Caring, not a hoot.

Time has passed, lots of years
    I'm back where I belong,
With caring family and friends
But it's taken so long.

Dream Platforms

Gliding silently, drifting so high
To ghostly platforms in the sky,
You may ask the reason why
    Do they stop or just float by?

Dreams, thoughts in black-and-white
Anchored ropes of starlight,
No logic to chart the flight
    Just wandering, un-contrite.

Erotically hovering in the mind
Let loose and completely blind,
To influences of any shape or kind
    Mundane tasks left far behind.

So whatever size the bed
A platform for the weary head,
Recharges energy that has fled
    And us, such dreams, enchanted.

The Story Weaver

The word story, true or fantasy
Is the bad start to any tale
However skilfully penned,
But can the writer depend –

On research, memory, talent
Joining up to illustrate
The facts with romantic flair,
Writing all with greatest care.

Although exaggerated
The story weaver with truth
To record for posterity,
The story, with due sincerity.

And so he weaves his story
Colouring his lines a bit
His characters risk jeering scorn,
As the story gets a little worn.

He may feel he can please the many
By annoying just a few
The unusual content of his work
Can be classified, merely as a quirk.

If he really gets down to writing
He can achieve a masterpiece,
Blending interesting fact or fiction,
Woven correctly, he creates an addiction.

Betrayed

I existed alone for many years
No one to share my world,
Pointless, every day the same
Too little laughter, too many tears.

I tried to forget my married life
Determined to carry on,
I did my best for family
I had been a caring wife.

You disagreed and left your home
You had a younger woman,
You broke up two families
And I was just left alone.

Did it matter that my father died
Not to you, of course,
You merrily bulldozed on
Your guilt shoved to one side.

It may sound a lot of twitter
I have good cause to feel,
Betrayed, ditched and cheated
No wonder I'm so bitter.

Others say I must be wrong
Little do they realise,
That one man caused such misery
And my memory is long.

Our Love

Our love is stronger than life itself
Stronger than jewels, gold or any wealth,
It will flourish in all life's stages
And endure throughout the ages.

Our love is future, present and the past
Our love is now and must surely last.
Our love bridges both old and new
It spans every scene and point of view.

Who dares to try and come between
A love like ours so firm and keen,
To demonstrate that we are certain
Our love can reach the final curtain.

When mortal life is snuffed right out
We may know what it's all about,
Our love will survive in its psyche form
As new, in another body, it is reborn.

The Fertile Mind

Why are some minds so appealing
  And some dull as tarnished brass?
Is it because they're anchored firmly
  To stay within their class?

Restricted by peers and parents
  Who ban such aspirations,
Keep in your place, my child
  Such ignorant stipulations.

But as the child grows older
  And the brain explores so fast,
Blossoming thoughts will prove
  All those restraints are past.

Thinking thoughts of better things
  Health, wealth and of fame,
The fertile mind insists that
  Life can never be the same.

Values will be established
  Deep, in inquisitive minds,
Demands for a better life
  For all individuals, unconfined.

Yet still, whatever education
  Is offered and received,
There remains those dull of wit
  Whatever the class perceived.

The Jackdaw

Seeking refuge he has made his home
    In the empty pointed steeple,
Towering high above the nave
Away from all the people.

On the rafters of the belfry
    Once hung the mighty bells,
Now all that moves each Sunday morn
Is he, a bird compelled.

He's constructed his platform nest
    A massive pile of sticks,
Lined with lichen, moss and fern
Ready for his chicks.

Right in the middle of this jumble
    Looking as just bits of litter,
He has placed shiny pebbles and glass
Chosen because it glitters.

Perfectly fit and aged in years
    Fearing he's left it too late,
He feels the urge to breed his kind
And seeks to find a mate.

He's sleek of plumage with beady eye
    For his female an outstanding match,
In the steeple he has a safe home
He proves a splendid catch.

Christmas

What does Christmas mean to you?
A time of peace and quiet,
Or, gorging, eating far too much
Shambles and a riot.

Fighting in the family
Kids too selfish to share,
Children pull and tug the toys
And parents don't seem to care.

Christmas is a celebration
Of the birth of Christ the Lord,
Not a time of grab it all
And gifts we can't afford.

Time of carols, sung and shared
A time of cards, crackers and tree,
The family unit joined as one
Enjoying the Nativity.

So, much to relax and celebrate
Taking it easy in favourite chair,
Thanks for a comfortable home
With a simply chosen prayer.

When It Rains

When it rains we have a gripe
 Cos day has turned dull and cold,
The whole of nature welcomes rain
 For plant life to unfold.

Rain makes the washing wet
 And busy housewife moan,
Now she has to transfer
 It all back inside her home.

Kids on picnics run for cover
 Sandwiches are soaked
Even pesky insects are wet
 And stop bothering folk.

Cricket match grinds to a halt
 As the rain stops play,
Stumps are drawn, the pitch is left
 To dry 'til another day.

Then the rainbow lights the clouds
 In resplendent coloured bands,
Shining but a moment brief
 Before fading over land.

When rain comes and breaks a drought
 On which our food depends,
'Tis the quantity helps grow our food
 From the hills to the Fens.

The Hanging Tree

Just outside the village confines
   Stands the ancient Hanging Tree
In reality a blasted oak
   That is there for all to see.

Grisly goings on that took place
   Where life was extinguished,
Branded thieves, peasants all
   Their death brought such anguish.

Hanged by the neck on a rope
   At whim of feudal lord,
Their only crime they stole to live
   For food they could not afford.

Fathers taken from their family
   No one left to provide,
Another fine example
   Of the great unfair divide.

So much owned by lord and master
   So little by toiling serfs,
They laboured hard dawn to dusk
   Nothing in their purse.

So, now and again one stole bread
   But that man's destiny,
Was suspension from the branch
   Of the dark Hanging Tree.

Hidden Treasure

The pirates tried to hide their hoard
    On islands remote and far,
They buried it deep and unseen
    Under the tropical stars.

They made a crude location map
    A guide to the treasure's site,
Very hard to decipher clues
    Made in the dead of night.

X marks the spot, the maps all say
    But where can one find X?
Most of the crews are long-time dead
    Cursed by the Captain's hex.

Some persistent seekers found
    A little of the treasure hoard,
Taking their lives in hand
    On beaches, and shores abroad.

Lacking both food and water
    Many perished in the search
When the aged map was wrong
    And left them in the lurch.

The treasure that is rarely hidden
    Is to be found at hand,
As comforts, pets and family
    Are not buried in the sand.

Prince and Darky

Prince and Darky they were called
Huge shire horses of many hands,
Who heroic tasks performed
    On my grandfather's land.

Darky was the smaller of the two
Coloured black and Prince was grey,
They ploughed the furrow as a team
    On heavy Bedfordshire clay.

Snug, fed and warm after work
In the stable they shared
One day when I went to look
    Darky's stall was bare.

I asked my dad where Darky was
All he said was he'd gone away
I expected to see him quite soon
    But there never was that day.

I found out much later on
He'd had a bloated gut,
The vet had to put him down
    No one heard the shot.

So Prince had to pull the carts
An old horse on his own
Put out to pasture for a time
    Reaping what he had sown.

His collar hangs in the stable still
Now both stalls are bare,
I wish I could go back in time
    And brush the horses there.

Equality
This Is a Personal Alternative View

Women expound all the time
About being as tough as males,
Don't they even realise
    That argument always fails?

On several counts, on battlefield
Perhaps get male colleagues killed,
By flinching in the fight
    If avoiding blood fresh-spilled.

They expect a man to rise and cede a seat
Why, he has equal right to sit,
Equal pay for equal work
    Yes, where appropriate.

In danger, should they expect a man
To rescue them from harm,
Putting his own life at risk
    By triggering an alarm?

Deceit, tears and temper
A woman's arsenal can,
If used to good effect
    Defeat a simple man.

Why not preserve the status quo
And leave equality alone?
A woman's talents will excel
    In kitting out the home.

Bargains

We buy and buy again
    Things we do not really need,
Is it because they appear value
    Or is it because of greed?

Will that still be around next week
    Or is it on the blink?
We hoard unnecessary goods
    It is the squirrel instinct.

To lay down stores for lean times
    To keep the pantry packed,
And never to reduce the heap
    We really should quickly act.

Bargains are not what they seem
    Just junk in thin disguise,
Stop the wasteful spending spree
    Become a little wise.

Grow up a bit, take careful stock
    Of cupboards, drawers, piled high,
Next time a product tempts you
    Think twice before you buy.

Situation Vacant

There will be a gap in her life
Were he to go away,
She would be cut in half, a zombie
    Not knowing night from day.

Did he really feel so sure
That his plotted course was right?
Or is it he wants to hurt her
    Before he takes his flight?

He was adamant and his point of view
Was as harsh as he knew how,
Hitting below the belt many times
    For she was only a stupid cow.

But she had deeper qualities
Than he could even dream,
Perhaps she'd fill the gap
    With another man to deem –

The situation vacant
Lasted only for a few hours,
She would make new friends
    Maybe love would flower.

Taking his place readily
With no more taunts and lies,
The female of the species
    Would regain her poise and pride.

Into Proportion

When things go wrong as they surely will
Temper any actions with great caution,
Think good and hard of consequences
    And get it all into proportion.

Is it worth it just to make a point
When a little thought will make you see?
Maybe there is a another view
    Stubbornness is sheer stupidity.

So, you are convinced you're right
And, therefore, others quite wrong,
The greater picture will reveal
    Single notes do not make a song.

Why get hold of the stick's wrong end
Jumping to hasty conclusions?
Is the other side really so bad?
    Abandon these daft illusions.

A short pause will pay great dividends
You will find the benefits galore,
By thinking through your acts
    And trying just a little more.

Don't take the moral high ground
Get things into perspective,
Your attitude and judgement
    Cries out for milder directive.

The Creator?

He had so much to do
    A myriad tasks to perform,
Thoughts conceived in distant space
    Just now were being born.

He needed to find an entity
    Whose power matched his own,
Her ideas, different to bring
    To share the immortal throne.

That part completed, He now turned
    To sifting dark from light,
Casting away the surplus gloom
    Creating slumber and night.

He thought of mighty, golden orbs
    To shine in heaven's firmament,
To stimulate the growth of life
    Provide all each was meant.

Full now with teeming life
    Abundant diverse creatures,
He turned His attention to
    A caretaker of all nature.

And so He created man
    A grave mistake of sorts,
Abandoned failed attempts
    Many prototypes aborts.

Finally, there came a being
    A little different from the rest,
A biped with basic reasoning
    This one appeared the best.

But did man really care?
    Only time will tell.
He abused his given world
    Turned paradise into hell.

By pollution, wars and crime
    He's ruined his habitat,
Cruel to the animals in his care
    There's no excuse for that.

The Creator now feels sad
    Cos his selected Creation,
Deserving the very worst of fates
    Is now due for extermination.

Just a Blade of Grass

A little green spike
Growing wild on the lea
    Hemmed in by many others
So very hard to see.

Lush and green grows the grass
And tall, until one hot day
    Our blade of grass becomes
Part of a bale of hay.

To nourish beasts for winter fodder
So the milk will still then flow,
    In spite of days of cold
With covering, sparkling snow.

The blade of grass has travelled far,
From field right through to hay,
    And in a cow's stomach waits
Not very long to stay.

Expelled in a sloppy mess
Back on to the very plot
    Where its adventures all began
As it roots in the same green spot.

Before Time

Before there was the earth
Before stars, planets and sun,
The concept of Creation
    Was in mind of the One.

That Being, that Entity
Who is all-omnipotent,
Could think and bring into force
    All diverse life on the continents.

The variety was so great
With ability to breed,
Life increased to the extent
    Too many mouths to feed.

Completely out of control
The numbers still increase,
The One will have to step in
    And think all life to cease.

So man has overstepped his mark
And caused his own demise,
By abusing his habitat
    With ignorance, greed and lies.

Is there a way forward we can go?
Stop all overproduction,
Only breed where there is food
    Avoid our own destruction.

Did the One fear this would happen?
Before man came into place,
Why not change His Creation
    And make of man a finer race?

St Swithin's Rain

When it rains it really rains
Stair rods spearing the ground,
Cascading on to the earth below
    A drumming, beating sound.

Leaves of trees drip constantly
Gutters overflow flooding out
Rain washes debris down the stream
    And down the water spout.

After days of rain we are quite fed up
The skies glower dark and grey,
We long for the rain to cease
    And clouds to go away.

Forty days of rain are predicted
At the time of St Swithin,
Henry VIII desecrated his shrine
    So rain drips upon his coffin.

The soil is saturated, can take no more
Will the rain ever stop?
Yet after a few weeks of drought
    We beg again for raindrops.

Gift of life for growing things
Plants need gentle lots,
But when it comes in bucket-loads
    It causes all to rot.

The Shortest Day

It's the shortest day of the year
Our sun is the furthest away,
Only light for few short hours
    Frost and ice holding sway.

Snow has fallen to decorate
The landscape both far and wide,
Veiled in glitter and shining through
    Decked in white a Christmas bride.

It's the shortest day, longest night
Nature's on holiday now,
Growth has ceased, food is short
    Ground too hard to plough.

Pagan festival to tempt the sun
To return to herald spring,
Warmer climes will ensure
    Fertility for everything.

Adapted from the pagan rites
Christian festival to remember,
We commemorate birth of Christ
    With Christmas in December.

The shortest day is soon passed
Darkness takes over the land,
But the long night of winter gloom
    Will fail to hold or stand.

Queen of Hearts

She chose to be Queen of Hearts
    Our princess, regally acclaimed,
Husband chose to play a different course,
Diana was her name.

Two fine sons she produced
    To give the throne some heirs,
Prince William is first in the line
Prince Harry too, proudly standing there.

Harry has proved to be stern stuff
    Doing well his share,
His mother was so innocent
Of the life that had no care.

There were rumours of an affair
    With a long-standing sweetheart,
He did not think or see
His marriage would fall apart.

Then in the Paris tunnel
    Hounded from door to door.
Diana's light was put out
Our princess was no more.

We miss her so and wish her back
    Alas that cannot be,
William and Harry soldier on
In spite of the tragedy.

I Walked in the Woodland

I walked in the woodland
Shuffled leaves under my feet,
 So many over the years
Had compressed to form soft peat.

Spongy to walk on
So gentle to my heels,
 Absorbing all the shocks
Refreshing, uplifting it feels.

Decay of old fallen trees
Had spawned varied fungi,
 Some too deadly to eat
Home to little blackflies.

From the death of the wood
New life is emerging well,
 Nutrients back in the soil
Feed roots, for spring bluebells.

A carpet of primrose, anemone, sorrel
Nodding, swaying to and fro,
 And dog roses pink and gold
Adorn the tall hedgerows.

Later the woodland rings
With call of thrush and dove,
 Whilst the skylark soaring high
Will kiss the clouds above.

The New Year

Two thousand and nine has gone
Into a new decade we enter,
A portent of things to come
    Our regrets, guilt trips all done.

This country brought low by fools
Mismanagement by those in charge,
Wasting our resources glibly
    Our soldiers without proper tools.

How can they face another year
Of the same old lame lies?
Give our boys our strong support
    And open up blocked ears.

Listen to the pleas for ceasing
The senseless occupation of Iraq,
Bring them back home at once
    New Year here would be pleasing.

We exist for so short a span,
And life takes many twists and turns,
We should kick out the traitors
    Who have ruined our fair land.

A New Baby

There is a new life on the way
The patter of little feet,
Bringing wonder, in our world
Our lives will be complete.

Be it boy or girl it matters not
A healthy child for us,
To be loved, and spoiled by some
The centre of all the fuss.

To grow up, stage by stage
Crawling, walking next,
A little bit of both of us
A chatterbox, complex.

Into this and into that
Curiosity second to none,
Investigating the kitchen bin
Rubbish is such fun.

Our little wonder learning much
From books, TV and school,
Like parents, learning all the time
When not to apply the rule.

There Comes a Time

There comes a time in our lives
Awareness of almighty power,
That's manifest in moon and stars
　　Directs the meteorite shower.

Master of all the universe
Controller of each and every day,
As birth takes place, and death occurs
　　We must comply, trust and obey –

The grand order of everything
Has laid out a primary plan
That directs our lives to be,
A learning curve for few of us
　　Who really want to see.

Nothing can change the order
Or alter the smallest part,
This power guides the progression
　　Of the stupid and the smart.

Our lives will run the same course
Whether we despair or rejoice
So, why do we like to say
　　That we may have a choice?

The March Hare

Cousin of the rabbit
Known as the March hare
Or character in a story
    At the moon they will stare –

When the time is right
Collectively they form
To gaze in mutual wonder
    Midnight until dawn.

This strange gathering
Is called a parliament
Just a friendly grouping
    Unlike a government.

Out in the green meadows
Antics they carry out
Gambolling head over heels
    What's it all about?

The welcomed coming of spring
The end of winter's hold
Nature's creatures breed
    Ignoring damp and cold.

Two hares have a boxing match
Upright on hindquarters
Fighting over a female
    Until one of them has caught her.

Not Alice through the looking glass
Not from a story book
An untamed, living animal
    Who at the moon does look.

The Old Windmill

Positioned high to catch the wind
The sails are spinning round,
The spindle shaft turns the stones
    And corn is quickly ground.

Serving folk in villages many
Dusty Miller is powdered white,
Flour-coated from head to foot
    Quite a ghostly sight.

A centre point and trading post
The windmill meets the needs,
Of bakers, cooks and the like
    With hungry mouths to feed.

One night lightning struck
The sails came crashing down
Now the top of the tower
    Has lost its working crown.

Repairs fast must be placed
Grain needs to be ground again,
Carpenters, joiners, steeplejacks
    Toiling long, hard hours sustained.

Finally the work was done
With the great sails whirling round,
Celebrations of great joy for
    The windmill has a new crown.

The Library Spirit

At end of a long hard day
 It is time to close the doors,
Evacuate the readers
Who've soaked up the lore.

Dusty books stand room-high
 Hiding a small host,
For behind the pillars and shelves
There lurks a captive ghost.

Long ago there was a fire
 Bomb damage in the war,
The child of the librarian
Was shut behind the doors.

A child who read many books
 Who never grew to man,
Now trapped in the library
As spirit pale and wan.

Many a library reader
 Has seen the little one
Clutching a book to read
A shadow quickly gone.

Memories of that dreadful night
 Haunt the library still,
The library spirit lingers there
Amongst the icy chill.

Another day dawns
 The library admits the crowd,
The people shuffle in
Greeting the spirit aloud.

180